Stepstones

Compilation 1

Excerpts from Readings Given to An
Al Miner & Lama Sing
Study Group

Stepstones – Compilation 1

By Al Miner and Lama Sing

Cover and book design by Susan Miner

Published in the United States of America

Library of Congress: 2015956672
ISBN- 978-1-941915-04-2

1. Lamasing   2. Psychic   3. Trance Channel   4. Consciousness
I. Miner, Al   II. Lama Sing   III. Title

For books and products, further information, or to write Al Miner, visit http://www.lamasing.net

The original intent of this book was to provide a collection to flip through for thoughts to ponder or meditate on that were taken from readings given for the Al Miner/Lama Sing Study Group.

These readings have emphasized that this is a living work, brought to us in this time of great change for our world: For those who are seeking to awaken to the Truth of their Being, we are at the apex of a profound opportunity during this time of heightened Consciousness and change. Therefore, this book is also for you, who are so awakening. Join us. We welcome you.

Al and Susan, and the Oneness Study Group

Notes:

Christ/the Master — "The Christ is a Principle. It is a Spirit. It is the life. The Master has brought this Christ Consciousness into oneness with Himself. Thus, He has become the Christ. Just so many stumble over this." —Lama Sing

Father — When Al and this work employ the term Father there is no implication of gender, humanness, or religiosity whatsoever, but simply a word to refer to, call on, and address in a deeply personal way the God Source, the Creator of All, the Beloved. Al has said, "If it's good enough for Jesus, it's good enough for me."

Words — "It is important that all who might read these words understand emphatically we are using words to describe some event and actualities that have no corresponding words in Earth. So we are using the best that is at hand." —Lama Sing

The Channel — This name is used throughout the book to denote the difference between Al, the man in finite form, and the part of Al that has left his form and is in realms beyond to channel the information. It is capitalized when used in place of his name.

Lama Sing — This name refers to an individual Al has known and worked with beyond and in this and other lifetimes. It also refers to the group, others who join Lama Sing to participate in gathering and offering information from Universal Consciousness in the readings.

Form — While in "pure" Consciousness no physical-like form is present, in some circumstances, being expressed in a form that appears physical is joyful and/or useful, both to Al in his experiences as well as to communicate an understandable narrative.

In Earth — When referring to life on Earth Lama Sing uses the term "in Earth" because he is referring to Earth as a realm of expression, similar to the common use of "in heaven."

Directly from the Lama Sing readings for this Project ...

We have asked our Brother, the Christ, to come forth, that He might honor us all... those who knowingly are a part of these works, and those who serve simply because their own spirit is encouraging them to so do. Let us join the Master, as He offers this blessing. Be mindful to receive it....

... He is touching you ...

Sweet Brother, we thank you for showing us the way, and for granting us Your healing grace and love unto all those who will hear the Call and answer it. So may it be.

You are the master of this journey. The power of all the others who have agreed enhances your mastery. †

When one can come together with a Group such as this, limitations that would otherwise seemingly be present will fall away. †

You are awakening the highest within you ... the beauty of God's touch that is You. †

The light of your Group is a call that is offered to all in each realm through which it transits, touching all in those realms in the center of their Being. †

You are choosing to *See*. In the Seeing, you will know your Self. In the knowing of Self, so do you know God. †

Seeing is the perception that has Knowing, a resonance within Self that brings a realization of what is being encountered. In that realization comes the potential for wisdom. The wisdom is the Knowing. †

The more you reach out to know that the others are intending with you, the greater is your potential power. The power grants you the awakening of your Authority. This Authority is your *true heritage*. †

As you realize that you have Authority, you will begin to manifest in accordance with that. †

The manifestation of your Authority will begin in small ways, so we encourage you to be alert. Observe and see the Authority going before you in activities and circumstances in your life. †

Learn to rest in the embrace of your Authority. Dwell upon this for just a moment here...
In resting in the embrace of your Authority you will discover something ... you are claiming Self. †

What is this Authority? It is God's thought of *You*. God's Love for You. It is the uniqueness of God's Word expressed as *You, through* You. †

Begin by realizing that you *can See*, that you *can Know*.

To do this with the Group brings together a bond of harmony of intent that brings the energy to a heightened level. This, then, resonates with Universal Law, which is God, and awakens the resonance of the uniqueness of God as expressed as You. †

Authority would be used in a loving way. As you use it in a loving way, you will find its potential expands. Use it, first, for self. Use your Authority to See and Know your Self to be that unique expression of God. In the Seeing and the Knowing of this, call upon the power gifted to you by the Master, the Christ, at the beginning of this work: His healing Grace. †

Let your Spirit hear the call and let it be amplified by the power of the Group, strengthened by the faith and belief held within each brother's and sister's Being. †

You have absolute – *absolute* – Authority over self. †

It is the nature of finiteness that this or that is the dominating force. But within You is the Authority, the power. Bringing this to the forefront of your consciousness is up to you. You must bring it forth.

In doing this, do not allow yourself to begin a series of evaluations... how well you are doing here and there. To do so is to affirm separateness, even the affirmation of separateness of yesterday versus tomorrow.

Believe in the present. Believe in your Authority. †

When the forces of habit and limitation try to call you back unto their embrace, immediately gift them with the Grace and Love of the Christ. †

If they receive it, you are the greater collectively for that; if they do not, you are freer because of that. †

The more you allow your consciousness to expand, to Know and See beyond the finite, so does your Authority expand along with that. †

You are awakening the Path within you. As you anchor this Path as a Group, the multitude can enter and depart via that pathway. †

Some from the realms of darkness move about the Earth influencing brothers and sisters, amplifying subtleties that otherwise might have been kept in moderation or in harmony.

We see the result of this as the rising of conflict of interest, challenges against belief, and so much more. As you see this, know that it is part of the convergence of the forces now present. Knowing this frees you from its potential impact or influence upon you. †

Your prayers are a blessing to those who are affected by those from the darkness. Your prayers not only contribute to the path of Light, but they conform to Universal Law, providing other benefits to the *light workers*, as they might be called. †

Know that you have the power of creation with *thought* and with *word*.

It is not only your deeds that create but the simple power of your words and thoughts. †

What you embark upon is within your dominion, your control, your Authority.

Others can support you, but you are the one who must do the work. And that is to free your Self. †

Honor your body as the living temple of God's choice of You within it. †

Hold, ever, a love of your Self in all that you do, if only just to honor the fact that God loves you. †

As we find the true joy and nature of our Being, that we are God's Creation, so Knowing, we express ourselves after the nature of our Creator. †

Freedom is that state of Knowing wherefrom there are no boundaries, no limits, no definitions, save those which are willfully chosen. †

The choices of some Children of God carry them into definition that is believed and loved, and thus, it *is*, and it becomes that which confines them.

It is in the confining that they engage in those activities that build understanding of the depth and breadth of their Freedom. †

Freedom is not an illusive quality to be sought after. It is already preserved within each soul. †

Freedom is the nature involved in making choices. When a choice is made based upon conditioned response, the Freedom involved is relative to the definition of the confines wherein that daughter or son of God might be found. †

Finding the full Knowing of Freedom from within an experience of definition becomes oft times challenging, not that someone is preventing you from attaining the Knowing of Freedom but that your *choice* limits the concept, the believability, of your true nature. †

Earth has its own beauty. This is God's presence, which gives life to existence.

In Utter Freedom, form would not be a part of the totality of Freedom. It would be a *choice* made *from Freedom.* †

It is possible to attain Utter Freedom while yet in physical form in the realm called Earth. It is possible if one believes. The believing comes from the (capital K) Knowing, the (capital F) Feeling, the (capital S) Seeing, and so forth.

What would you do with that Freedom? †

You would love – *utterly* – the realm of Earth if you were totally, utterly Free. You would love every aspect of it. You would see no good and bad, only the beauty of the opportunity, from Utter Freedom, to willingly express the choice to experience. †

If you arrive at Complete Freedom while yet in physical form, your love *could* be a boundary. It could be, in effect, a definition, a perimeter.

But then, if you were utterly, truly Free, that would be impossible, for True Freedom is Knowing as God Knows. †

Freedom ... If one loves a certain type of food, is it difficult to give up that love of that food? Is it difficult to break a habit that you have become fond of? If you love someone and they do not love you back, is there a difficulty in that, an imbalance? Freedom ... †

What is love, after all? Is love a state of being that flows freely to and fro and is exchanged without qualification or definition? Is love the same yesterday as it is today and will be tomorrow?

Love is qualified in the Earth in so many different ways, and if we qualify something, have we not limited it, defined it? In a way, bound it? †

Can a group, if they agree to a common singular intent, achieve that intent? Would there be the ability of a group to be united in what they believe to be Freedom? Can the *group* release any limitation or any love of a certain state of being? It is not to imply that they cannot, ultimately. In the moment, True Freedom is not something that can be recalled from the wellspring within. First there must be the Freedom for self. †

Sustenance of all things in the Earth realm is interdependent upon one another and upon the realm itself. To break Free from this is no small issue, because the multitude who are present love the realm called Earth and their choices. †

In the confines of structure comes the feeling of familiarity, comfort, the ability to know through definition. Without these confines or structures, many would feel, quite literally, lost. †

You can attain Utter Freedom. When you reach the point of Utter Freedom, it is probable that you would choose not to violate the love of the choices of the others around you. If a *group* reaches Total Freedom, it is possible that they can create an environment that can exist within the embrace of the realm of Earth, yet not violate the love of others. It does seem unlikely to most all, and yet it is possible. †

When Jesus walked on the Earth, He made Himself one with all that was. He was able, through His Love and Grace, His Oneness with God, to unify with whatsoever was before Him ... including the process called death. †

Christ honors all, is one with all, and He sees death merely as a pathway to move to the next existence. †

Utter Freedom is seen by many in your Group as only being attained after the transition from the finite body. †

You are choosing to reach for a united intent of Freedom. Whether that Freedom is in the *Ultimate* sense while yet in finite form in the Earth is within the choices, the hands, of those who seek it. †

It is possible for Utter Freedom to coexist within the defined.

Freedom would come about through the gradual realization of the fruits of claiming same: that conditions of dis-ease would begin to dissipate, that hunger would begin to vanish as abundance became beautifully apparent, and so forth. †

That one who has an attitude of Loving Neutrality within themselves begins the process from that moment of releasing any aspects of lack of ease. They begin to dissolve old habits that are limiting to them. They begin to open themselves to receive the gifts of God that have, in many cases, long awaited their reception. †

Authority means to claim Honor for Self and God within: the Truth of who you are and your eternal nature. †

Anchoring the Path is the claiming of the Unlimited nature of Self.

All that is being discussed here is for the awakening of Self. It is to set Self Free. †

Within the individual who is Awakened and claiming the Christ Consciousness of Self, there are no constructed aspects of self that can divert or limit the power of prayer. †

When the Master walked upon the Earth as the man called Jesus, His mere presence resonated. Some were fortified with the multitude of veils or sheaths and their attitude (we might actually call it intent) was so diverse from the Master's Love and Compassion that, while they felt a stirring within, they chose their own intent. †

You will know when you've Freed yourself when you see all things in the nature of the perfection that is at the core of their Being. †

Your life force, in other words God's intent that is You … If you do not recognize that this is the Center of who and what You are – and do so in the fullness of loving that Center and knowing that it is righteous because God has placed this here – it would be difficult for you to truly set yourself Free. †

True Freedom lies within you. It must pass through veils of separateness, judgment, habit, fear, and so forth, and these are like mutations upon the beauty of who and what you are. So to truly love Self means that you must go within and seek out this Center and allow yourself to feel it and know it.

When you can repeatedly look at yourself in the looking glass and state, *I am a beautiful Child of God, uniquely created out of God's Love for me. I* [your Name] *love You,* and it flows in genuine truth that you do love the image, then you are setting yourself Free. †

The thought-forms of limitation that exist in the world around you are mutations upon the Truth. When you have set yourself Free, you will see these as a collage of individual or collective choices, but you will know the beauty of the creative potential of God that has given these Children the right to create and to manifest this creation. †

It is good to understand the nature of *doing.* Are you *doing* something when you pause and intend something? Are you *doing* something when you go to your sacred place? Are you *doing* something when you call the names of your group?

You see? It is good to affirm, "I *do* this in God's Name." So doing, you and God are one in the doing. †

You are a part of the eternal Life Force of God, which you bring to focus upon that one or those whom you've placed in the center of your work.

When you do this after calling the names in your Group – and, incidentally, it is important for all of you to think of your Group as a continuous circle when you call the names ... unbroken, unending – when you call the names, you invoke the power and uniqueness of each of these brethren. And this forms a circle of envelopment that is Lovingly Neutral because all have agreed to offer their love and prayer as a gift to one another with no strings, no attachment, no hidden agenda, so to say. †

Asking for prayer is like opening your front gate into your property. See? †

It may seem curious at first to think of Loving Neutrality as *giving* something, but doesn't it? If someone is dis-eased and you give them the ease that is found in Loving Neutrality, that is a gift to them.

There is great potential in the attainment and the enactment of Loving Neutrality. †

Tools are valuable in varying degrees and gradients for various different Children of God. Some find that the presence of tools is an adjunct to increasing or amplifying their intent, their faith, so to say.

Do you *need* the tools? No. But if they help you, then, they are of value to you. †

Authority is the power that unleashes all of the beauty of your Uniqueness. It is the Authority to claim mastery over each limitation that you might find. †

Use your Authority with the loving Compassion of the Christ, and that Compassion will embrace you and will expand from the Center of your Being like radiating beams of a rainbow reaching out to touch the next energy and the next. †

The journey through life and mass-mind thought provides the triggers to help you find any subtle limitations. †

Remember Oneness: What is done to one impacts all; what is done to many impacts all with even greater force. †

The question was asked how to see things in Loving Neutrality in events that are extremely challenging such as racism or cruelty....

When you See with your complete Sight, you See that all things are appropriate in their place and in accordance with the choices and intentions of *all* of those who are involved. This does not moderate the effect or the event. It is to see as God sees: that these are His Children and they are journeying in the depths of experiences. Some of these Children make choices that are based upon conditioning that they have endured in the journey to that point. Some of the Children who are experiencing these challenges have asked to enter in, knowing they would be steeped with prejudice or such that would cause them to react.

This is a journey. You may choose, just as they, and your choice in these works brings a light to show that their choices are not in harmony with who they are.

The more of you who can bring your Light to the forefront by setting yourselves Free, by Anchoring the Way, the greater will the Light be seen and felt. And those who feel it may call themselves to the forefront from within and release that to and by which they have been conditioned, and reach beyond the sheaths of that conditioning to find Truth.

If you let your Sight See beyond that which is at the forefront, beyond the sheathing, you will know these to be brothers and sisters struggling to find themselves. †

It is good to make a distinction between choices and choosing versus judgment.

You make choices about what to eat, what to wear, where to go on a day off from work if you are working, and so forth. Those are not the same as judgment. †

Judgment of another or of a state of being has a power behind it that is drawn from the wellspring of self. When one makes a judgment, they are placing their life energy in line with that judgment, so that the line of light between that decision to judge and self is a continual nourishment of that judgment. This is one reason why hatred and bigotry and bias and all those sorts exist, because the lines of light from within continue to nourish them. And all those who have attached a judgment in past are nourishing that judgment.

In order for that to conclude, there must be the realization and the *freeing* of the judgment, just as you would free a creature that you have penned. When you free the judgment, not only do you get your good energy back, but the thing that was being judged is unburdened.

The more who can set their energy free and unburden others, the greater is the burden relieved, released, and the prejudice dissipated. †

In the face of challenge, know the Truth.

In the power of Faith, many things can be wrought; in the power of Faith by one who has claimed the Christ Consciousness within, *anything* can be wrought. †

In the Knowing, comes the Awakening. In the Awakening, the Faith is called to the forefront. Then all else is subjugated (in a manner of speaking), placed in abeyance, and the Faith becomes the Light, the Power, the Force, that goes before. †

Freedom tastes like Honey. It is sweet. Freedom feels like a soft garment that rolls like velvet. Freedom smells like a fresh field full of flowers. Freedom feels like a bird lazily soaring in flight. Freedom sounds like the water singing to you as it trickles down, cascading over rocks and stones and such. Freedom feels like the unbridled energy pouring forth from a child.

Freedom is the love of everything. Freedom is the spotlight that shines out to help you see that your intention is reachable and guides you along the path to its attainment. †

Jesus loves the little children. He does so largely because He knows they are entering pure and that they are given the opportunity to serve their intent.

Whether it is to fulfill a role in the part of another's choices (often referred to as karma) or whether it is to forge ahead in the awakening of their own spirit's completeness, He feels and sees the love of Life, Itself. †

We have spoken of sacred "places."

You are the ones who make these places Sacred. When you do, the power of Life Itself awakens to your call of being Sacred. This power is awakened and remains, so that others who are sensitive to same who come across this place (if it is a location) will feel, will pause a moment and feel a rush of energy, a vibration or some such. It is you who is calling forth the beauty of Life that is expressed in all that is.

Continue where you can to make sacred times in your day. Make these times so very special that you long for them to arrive. (They should not be necessarily rigid, you see, just your choice to make this or that time Sacred.) In moving into those times/spaces that you deem as Sacred, when you do this for self you are doing it for the entire Group.

If you choose, like so many do, to pause at twilight and celebrate the glory of the day, to give thanks for the gifts of the experiences that have been a part of it, merely loving the experiences for the gifts they give to you, hold the Love from within Self outward in outstretched hands, literally or figuratively, and offer this to your beautiful world. †

What you offer to the world, you offer to God, for God is the Creator.

What you offer to yourself by loving self and casting out judgments of self, Freeing limitations and setting self Free, you do this for God within you ... a change of the thinking to See all things as beautiful opportunities, and making that so by *choosing*. †

We have in past emphasized twilight, for it is the time of movement of spirit on the land in a way of rest. All that is *alive* (in your nomenclature of the Earth) on or in the Earth has a time of rest, and their spirit soars.

You can soar with this beautiful energy in the oncoming darkness of twilight. The dance of lights in the sky, the sounds of the creatures calling out to wish one another a good journey during their slumber ... all this and so much more is yours for the taking. Choose it, and choose it often.

You can use the dawning in the same way, to give thanks for that which is to come, knowing that as you do, the greater will be yours. †

Many prayers are offered each day to each of you in the Group. Honor those who give them by pausing to receive. In the receiving, the giver receives many, manifold over because you have completed the pathway of the prayer's movement. When you receive, it flows from you on to the next and the next, and the Circle will rise and all of you will find yourselves celebrating the joys of one another's accomplishments. †

You will feel and see the light of hopefulness, and you will look above that which has chosen to wallow in darkness of illusion. But life is eternal, so as we have spoken before, pray for those who have lost their way as an offering of your Light flowing from the Center of You within. As you do this, the Christ will take your hand and walk with you to touch them. †

It is upon the wings of God's Love that we can all journey forth unto that which is calling to us. As we do, we shall Know that, within us, this same Love ever is present. And in the knowing of this, we will be the channels through which God gives it. †

We heard an outcry from some in the shadows who received the Love of the Christ and cried out that they were unworthy. As they shrank back into the shadows, our brothers and sisters went to them and spoke to them: "Do not lament. Thou art worthy. His gift of Love is always offered to you. Receive it now."

What is the nature of one who is lost? Who has burdened them so, that they feel unworthy? From whence cometh the energies that surround them and sheathe them with the illusion of unworthiness and greater? Who would cast such a thought to a brother or sister? Who? †

When you see those who do not act in accordance with the Law of God but are conversely following, as is their right, their free will choice, and you know these choices to be against thee and against that which is the known righteousness that you hold within, can you offer them God's Love? Or will you send them the energy that will bind them, that will sheathe them in the guilt and sorrow of their deeds, that they cannot know and see the Light of God within when this journey in which they have wronged another is concluded? †

Whenever you see anger, betrayal, acts of war, of violence, if you contribute like in kind to those, the result is the strengthening of that energy.

If you meet such challenges that are personal to you in a spirit of loving righteousness, in honor and the upholding of the Law, this is of an entirely different nature. But do not be at a distance sending hatred or anger, for you open yourself to receive those energies upon that same pathway. †

All live within the body of God. If that is a true statement, then what in the body of God would you ever hold anything but Love for? †

You gathered your group to form a Circle of loving prayer and, within that intention, you grew to know one another and to love one another in a way that exceeded your previous knowing. This is still growing.

Now we encourage you, only an offering, when you speak the names of your sisters and brothers, do so with renewed vigor, with renewed dedication now that you are seeking to set yourself and them Free. And notice the brilliance that you feel from each one as you allow your thoughts to rise above the finite definition into the infinite potential. †

Pause before you begin speaking the names and seeing your brethren, and think of your own name. They are all going to speak your name!

How will you receive the gifts they offer you? †

You are gifted with the greatest of all gifts: the simple right of choice. Your Authority is the power that enables you to exercise that choice. †

Feel the wonder of it. Feel your group rising. Not in a sense as a cloud would rise on the horizon, but *rising in the awareness and claiming that you are His!* †

You are not an idle, biological evolution or such. You are the intent of God to *Be* you. †

As your Circle of intent continues to rise, it will meet that which has been prepared for you here. Then choose again to make this one. And the Way will be opened, and the path, within you, will be anchored. †

Many of you have stood steadfastly in service to others as they have presented needs. In this beautiful Group and its works over the Earth years past, The Watch[1] has been kept.

Henceforth, as you begin your prayer, create the sacred Consciousness – sacred because all of you hold it in an attitude of reverence, joy and love. Now, as you do that for a moment before your prayers begin, *you will feel His presence*. If you do not, we say to you quite simply and lovingly, do it again, and open yourself. †

Never let your heart be weary in the face of that which is of finiteness. Rather, fill your heart with the Knowing that He dwells therein with you. He is that Loving Force that will lift you up whensoever there is the need. You have only but to ask and to open yourself. †

You may see acts, deeds that do not bear the Light that is within the doer, the nature of love and truth that is at the core of each sacred teaching. See these only as leaves in the wind for the times upon the Earth when it shall be as such. †

What if one of those you've known a lifetime or two ago is in dire circumstances, punished, tortured for vile acts in this lifetime because they are striking out against that which they themselves cannot even name? Would you feel for them anger? Hatred? Or would you remember the love you held for them in that past time?

Bring Jesus before you when next you consider such things and ask Him: "What think You, Brother?"

He might say to you, *When the twilight comes of all of these experiences which others adjudge, we will be there to take their hands and lead them into God's Love for them. They will bear no weapons, no scars, no hatred, no remorse, no guilt, no sins, for all of these are of finiteness.* †

Spirit is the pattern of the true beauty of the soul. It is the creation of God. †

As you join in the sacred Circle and breathe the breath of God with each name you speak, perhaps you will reach your own Spirit. And perhaps so doing you will *believe*. This is our eternal prayer for you. †

You are about a good work, dear brothers and sisters. Treat it with compassion and with the knowing that it is Truth. †

Do not shy away from that which seeks to claim you in habit. These are no more than items of clothing worn on a journey. Lay them aside, for they have served their purpose. But you, you and your Group, have begun a new journey, a journey of the uttermost potential of True Freedom.

Lay aside the old garments now, not later but now. †

You are His and He is yours. In your words, in your thoughts, your deeds, every step that you take, remember this, and the way will open for you.

You are God's miracle. †

You are beyond definition, even beyond explanation. You are greater than emotion or mind. Emotion and mind are the tools with which your soul extends its spirit forth to do works of understanding and service. †

Love your bodies in the manner as Jesus loves the temple and acted to cast out the dis-ease of that which would defile the temple with deliberateness and with love. †

You do not give a thirsty man sand to drink; you give him water. You do not give one who perpetuates darkness and limitation more darkness and limitation; you transcend their illusion, show it for what it is. It is then for them to take of the water or nay. †

Within Jesus, then and now, is our Father. Who is within you, if not the same? †

Begin each day with the *knowing* that it is a gift. Whatso'er comes upon the energies borne in that day, see it in this way and that will be your harvest. The day and the energies therein are yours. *You* decide whether they are a blessing or nay by what you carry away from that day's ending. †

Pause before slumber and gather the harvest of the day just concluding and celebrate each aspect of the harvest. You are the master of the harvest. †

If you think with intensity upon a grain of sand, it becomes a boulder in your path. But if you place it in its proper accord, it makes your pathway just that much firmer. †

The Peace of God is yours, for you are His. Think on these things and be, in this time, known as His. †

Whenever there is the quest for knowledge, for truth, there comes to the forefront the uniqueness of the individual who is seeking. When there are many who gather together, such as your Group, the intent to quest for Truth, for Understanding, blossoms because of the uniqueness of the Group itself.

Feel the uniqueness and the perspective that each has and is offering to the center of your Circle. And as the energy grows and expands, there is the opportunity for you, each one, to do the same. †

Have no boundaries, have no percepts. Believe in that which you Know that comes to you in the realization that, as you have opened yourself, when the energy seeks to fill you, it is our Lord God's intent to fill you that you might be that full cup from which you can give to others. †

Recognize that, in the present, Consciousness is awakening in the expression of finiteness at a level that it has not for some considerable Earth measure. This has afforded you considerable latitude and potential.

Cast aside the structure, and know that you are an instrument of God without boundary, without definition, with the exception of your beautiful uniqueness. †

Be open to the discoveries that you are now making, for these will afford you the greater opportunity to be of service, just as when the Master walked in the Earth as the man Jesus. †

All of the energy centers are involved in the progression of one's consciousness. But this has to do with the interaction of the energy centers with the finite expression and the Spirit as it is seeking to be involved with that finite expression.

The Consciousness of Self has no such limitation. †

The Consciousness of Self is opening and the effect that you are feeling, each of you in your uniqueness, has to do with that Awakening. †

Spirit, mind, and body ... These are thought of in the singular sense because of their uniqueness. Consciousness does not recognize them as separate. Consciousness Sees and Knows in a state of Oneness. †

True Freedom cannot be based upon the outer. True Freedom is an inner accomplishment and attainment. When you are Free within, the outer will follow this. †

There must be an inner joy, the state of Knowing that you are ever One with your Creator. In this Knowing, there will come that flow of Consciousness that is a realization that the outer is the product of the inner Light, the inner belief.

As you believe in your nature as an eternal Child of God and you find joy in the moment, the moment that follows will produce a result after its kind. †

Do not struggle against burdens, for this gives them energy. There is no burden outwardly that cannot be found internally as some neglect, some sense of ignoring the true nature of your Being. †

As matters of challenge come before you, do not give them energy after their kind. Rather, give them your peace and your honor. †

Your ultimate goal will be the emergence, the unification, of the spiritual with physical, a point in your progression where no barriers stand between you in physical and in spiritual. †

Journeying into the Earth is a healing intent. Your healing is a part of the gift that you give to the Earth.

Healing is that which is sought after, for healing is the relationship between that which is Known and the unknown, to give the understanding that can be gained through journeying in a sense of finite definition. †

You are an eternal Creation of God. Even as you know this in your current mind, you also know that you are in a physical body. When there can be the realization that the physical body is by choice and that it is in harmony with the structure of the realm in which it is expressed, you begin to realize the power that you have by knowing this. This knowing comes about by realizing first and foremost that you are a Child of God. †

When the choice is to seek Truth, you begin the process of Freeing yourself; when you are comfortable in that which is familiar or gives you reference points, boundaries, you are not seeking Truth. †

It is possible to have no boundaries and yet be in finite form. Whether or not one wills this, chooses it, is up to the individual. †

You are eternal Creations of God in a journey in finiteness. The true realization of this will set you Free and accomplish the abolishing of separateness. †

There has come an indicator of the rapidity with which the energies are in motion. The changes are taking place in regard to the consciousness of the Earth in general, and other associated realms to be sure. This is a profound opportunity. †

For this particular work of raising the consciousness of the entire Group in a unified way, we would focus on the individual and the uniqueness that God intends for that individual. †

Your work and the work of other groups similar to yours, and individuals as well, contribute to the mass-mind thought and the collective consciousness that surrounds the Earth.

Where you are at present is very significant. There has been a progression of measurable noteworthiness, not only in the sense of the individual consciousness and its potential for receptivity and awareness, but in the groups and classes and masses. This has been foretold by many in millennia past: that during this particular period of time there would be a window of opportunity that can be used by those who are seeking to set themselves Free and to contribute that Consciousness to mass-mind thought.

This potential can raise the entirety of mass-mind thought and the realization that while there is the experiencing of finiteness, physical body and such, there is the eternal nature, the eternal Self that is always present. This is being awakened.

What lies ahead is in the hands and minds, hearts and spirits of the Children of God incarnated in the Earth. There are other forces involved, pure energy, great cycles that come into confluence periodically from the force of the Word of God. They are intended as a part of the Love of Father that flows constantly. These cycles include other realms besides the Earth, and other levels of consciousness that are not finite.

So you are facing an opportunity to not only set yourselves individually and collectively Free, in the sense of not being bound to limitations, but also to contribute to the overall consciousness of your realm, which has a domino effect upon associated realms, including those realms unto which entities journey upon departure through the process you call death. †

The Consciousness of the individuals involved in the Group has to do with the acceptance of their own Uniqueness and also their own Oneness with God. †

There was just recently what you could consider a knock upon the window that was a burst of Consciousness that came about as the result of many different entities at work seeking to Free Consciousness. It is not unanticipated and it should be expected to continue through, and perhaps even beyond, the period demarcated as 2018.

The bottom line here is that you have gathered together at this time because you have felt an inner calling. Those of you who have felt this calling are probably hearing the call more clearly than some of the others who are not so vibrantly stimulated by this opportunity at the onset. †

The most powerful force you have lies within you. It is the presence of your Creator, the Force that is within and about all that is. †

If you recognize yourselves as part of all that is, everything, it is like opening the door to the chamber wherein God is within you. †

The Freeing of yourself is that you would set aside habit that is limiting and that you would think in terms of there being an ever-present potential and holding joy within you. †

It is possible for you to move within Universal Law as it is expressed in the Earth in a harmonious way, a Lovingly Neutral way, where you are intending no thing, merely honoring and loving one another, which is, after all, honoring and loving God by way of the expression of those individuals. †

True Freedom has no limitation. Therefore, for you to have True Freedom, would you expect to hold on to one single limitation? †

Freedom means that all things about you and within you are Freed. The moment you reach that point of absolute Freedom, then all is yours.

The paradox of this is that, as you are willing to give all things their Freedom, all things wish to be one with you. †

You can love things but not need them. The love for them is as the open-handed holding of a beautiful bird; the need for them is the clenching of that hand. †

From Loving Neutrality you can See, you can Know. If you do not have Loving Neutrality, you cannot tell whether your hand is opened or closed, because the part of you that is not Lovingly Neutral will color that. †

Truth is within you. If you wish to color over the Truth, there are many thought-forms available in the Earth that will nourish that wish. Very popular among them is guilt, sorrow, remorse. These are the opposite polarities of True Freedom. †

If you feel a need to love someone because there is an emptiness within you, that is an imbalance. If you feel a love for something, someone, because you see its beauty and you simply uphold it for its beauty, your hand is open. But you must be able to turn away from that which is loved in such a manner and move on. If your love of a thing or person is such that you cannot turn away from it, then that is a limitation.

If you are willing to See and to Know, then you will realize that the Truth of Love is Freedom, *absolute* Freedom. †

Everything within the creation of God interacts. Therefore, your actions, your thoughts, your words, your deeds all contribute to the energies that are in motion. †

Energies are constantly shifting about within the body. The DNA, as it is called, is thought of as consistent and specific. The specificity of it is constantly under modulation by the energies in which it is formed. †

The evolution of consciousness is ordered. That is a part of the structure, the Universal Law, presently in place within your realm. If the consciousness is raised, the level of application of Universal Law will also modulate. Not that the Law isn't perfect. You would simply feel a different reaction from it. †

Ever should there be held in the mind and heart in any journey the affirmation that God journeys with thee. Knowing this and affirming it brings to the forefront of any journey's events the understanding of whatsoever shall be met upon that path. †

Let us oft pause to give a blessing of Peace to any and all who are struggling with that which is unknown, that which is challenging, and that which is seen in the present time only as a burden. †

In embarking on a journey to find the true nature of Self, build within the joy for Self, the recognition that you are a beloved Child of God.

The relevance of your Spirit to the opportunity that lies ahead is not to be taken lightly. So we encourage you to know the depth and breadth of God's love for You:

It has no ending.

Even though you have heard these words and this message many times in past, we repeat it here because of that information that is about to be given.

[August 8, 2015] ...

Many of you have noted shifts in energy, an expansiveness that has seemingly no real definition. This has to do with the movement of the cycles of energies and the result of choices involving many of your brethren. These brethren, who have been dwelling in various levels of consciousness, progressed by their united choice to seek and claim Freedom. The impact of this has sent a joyful ripple throughout Consciousness.

The energy of the accomplishment of these brethren is a gift to all of Consciousness. This is a flow of energy that could be clearly described as the Consciousness that is aligned with the Christ. As such, there has been a reaction on the part of those forces that seek to limit that kind of change. These reactive forces have their own right under the Law of God to express themselves when confronted with such a surge of the Light. This has been taking place more subtly, but reached a pinnacle in the days around this event.

For those are seeking to Free themselves from limitation, this provides greater energy. The pathways that have been blazed by those who have gone before you are now much more luminous and notable than you might have perceived them in past.

You will find your *energy* to be much more brilliant spiritually, and may be noted on the part of those whom you meet. You may be much more able to determine the nature of those you meet and whether or not they are in harmony with your intent.

This is a part of the expansion of Consciousness that is taking place in this "window of opportunity" that is a part of the confluence of these cycles as has been predicted from long ago through to your current.

As you choose to Free yourselves in a manner that has been more difficult in past, you may find the Light seeking to lift you much more than just shortly ago. †

All throughout that which is, is the Light of God giving it existence, providing it the opportunity and right to be. †

The right to *Be* and the differentiating nature of the intent of those individuals and groups who are choosing to return to their true nature, who are choosing to break Free from the limitations woven into the pattern – the mass-mind thought-form prevailing in the Earth – will create a heightening of the energies.

In accordance with the Law, you will see more evidential, noteworthy reactions on the part of the "balancing forces." But in the window of this opportunity, the Light has made a great foothold according to the choices of the Children of God within those confines who are seeking. †

As one who is dwelling within the Universal Law expressed in a realm of finiteness calls out unto God in an attitude of righteousness, bearing no intent other than to bring harmony, that call is honored. †

If there is the choice for the darkness of illusion to be perpetuated, those who carry the Light within and without take this Light to those are seeking it. Then as one might awaken within the darkness of illusion, the Light is there for them. †

You are beginning a new cycle of consciousness, not just because of the shifts of consciousness in the adjacent realms, but because the energies that you have put forth are having an effect. †

Your Circle is rising in the consciousness that envelops the Earth. So as your Circle raises its consciousness, and the gift of Love and the sweet Peace is offered to each name as you speak it, as you hold it within, the entire Circle is blessed. These blessings collectively elevate the consciousness of all within the Circle. †

Those of you who are approaching this work in an attitude of idleness, we encourage you to step up and be more focused and serious, humbly given. For this opportunity, were you to see it from here, is most assuredly one you would not want to be idle in. †

The energies of those who are in the forefront of the Group effort are profoundly blessed, for your dedication is being received as beams of your loving intent radiate outward unto the many who gather to observe this Circle of loving light as it is moving through consciousness. †

You are a clear, defined, expression of your intent. This expression is having a reaction to those who are dwelling in the shadows. With renewed focus and even more of your Love, you might now begin reaching out to those who are hiding in the shadows. †

If you encounter one or more dwelling in the shadows, claim your righteousness as a Child of God and under that Authority grant them forgiveness. The greater you are willing to do this without hesitation, the greater is your Group granted, even moreso, the greater blessing. †

The righteousness is yours, as a Child of God, to answer the calls, and the Master stands beside you to so do. Do, then, as He would do. See? Do no less than this. Mark you: *do no less than this.* †

Think of the power of the Authority of a Child of God as the signet of Righteousness that is yours and claim your Heritage. †

Carry this Authority with you in your prayers. If a call comes to you, answer it from that position of Authority. †

In order that your Authority does not surge forward and undo that which is not seeking to be undone, employ the Authority with gentle Love and Peace. But if a small voice within the masses calls out to you, note that you clearly have the right to answer. As you answer, do so unwaveringly with the Authority that is your Heritage. †

Carry your Authority a few steps further. Use it in your daily life to see with a new Sight, to build Understanding in your heart and mind. †

Seek a unification of your Consciousness with the finite expression you have in this current incarnation. †

Many of the Angelic Host have been coming in greater number because the intent of your Group and others like you is so noteworthy that it is making awide a path of Light, a path of Light that can be used for the Messengers of God to move easily in harmony with all that is in answer to your intention. †

As we journey forth upon the Word, place Peace before you, for the Peace that goes before is as placing God's Will before you. †

Many souls cry out in the darkness of illusion in the pain of not-knowing, the pain of fear, and literal pain borne in the physical body. The more you cleave unto the unification of your Group intent, the greater is the potential to reach these. Some would call them lost souls. We see them as beloved brothers and sisters who are striving to Awaken. Join us in reaching out to them, so as it brings you joy. †

Look upon the enemies of your country and see them as the Children see them. Look upon yourself as the Children see you. †

This is a time wherein the opportunity is, yes, quite profound, but there is always the opportunity for the individual and the groups to gather together to choose their path, individually and collectively, to Freedom. †

Those of you who are at a distance can offer power to those individuals who have the opportunity to make the change, and that is precisely what you are about. †

It is not only your own Spirit that walks about giving to others. Since you have gathered together with your Group, their spirits are combined with you, and the greater force is that their willingness is to serve with you and with the Spirit of God. †

Never forget, the most powerful force you have at your command is prayer. The power of your prayer, when you are Awakened, is as that of the Christ. †

All of God's Children have the right of free will choice. Whether dominated or dominators, all involved have free will choice. To take an action against what is occurring is to presume that you know what their choice should be. †

We are all petals upon the Great Flower which is God. That which rolls off of us is just so as the rains upon the petals of a flower in Earth ... it rolls to the center. The Center is God, wherein all things are brought into harmony in "God's time." God's time is according to the free will choices of those who are involved. †

Meet that which is in opposition without giving to it the energy that it is seeking to perpetuate itself. Violence begets violence; love begets love. †

Mind and Spirit are not in opposition. As mind goes about discovering itself, it will come to know that it is the instrument of Spirit. In other words, mind and Spirit are one. †

A question was asked about the Hadron Collider. The Hadron Collider cannot be taken over by opposing forces any more than your automobile engine could be taken over by them (though, with a note of loving humor, some might say theirs has been). †

The forces that would seek to oppose have no great potential. They have only their collective choice and the history of choices made. It is this collective *choice* that is seeking to sustain itself. †

You are the Children of God. The Hadron Collider is merely a creation of your combined spirits ... yes, *your* combined spirits. For if you believe that the scientists involved in the creation of the device are separate from you, then you are nourishing the opposing forces.

Your Spirit *helped* to create the device; your Spirit is helping the scientists to ultimately discover their Oneness with God. †

You are seeking to balance, not so much so good against evil, but habit on the one polarity and Consciousness on the other. †

You can give to those who are questing, but you cannot give to those who are not questing. †

There is no right or wrong. †

Reach out in heart, mind, and Spirit before any word comes forth from your mouth. As you do this, see all in the Love that you feel within and the way will open for you. †

Your Group is rising in Consciousness. There are some who are on the periphery, but the energy and the intent of the Group at its core is sufficient that all are involved and equally blessed as a result. †

Each one in your group – see, *each one* – who takes a step has taken that step for all the others. †

If you attain Consciousness, it is yours. The only way it can be set aside is if you choose to so do. †

Those who have actively sought and have, through their accomplishments and choices, reached a level of Consciousness wherein they are, to varying degrees, essentially Free, their Freedom has enabled them the choice: they could depart from the physical body or continue their tenure in the Earth. †

Awakening does not come about in every instance by a great happening on the outer, but by a gentle realization that occurs and grows from within to without. †

There are children who recently departed the Earth. If you wish to know them, go in your meditation to that place where you would find laughter, and you will find them. Think of the children as wanting to bring to you the Love and Laughter that is the Truth of Spirit.

In realms beyond, Laughter is sought after because it is an expression of Love for God. As one descends into greater and greater realms of expression – in other words, where expression becomes more predominant (*form*, that is) – the laughter seems to have less and less resilience. The children are seeking to rekindle Laughter in and about the Earth. If you welcome them, they will give it to you. See? †

There is one Spirit, and you are all a part of It. You know yourselves in the separateness as God has intended you, yet you cannot take a cup of water from a well and say, "It is not of the well, it is of somewhere else." True? You are of the waters of Spirit. †

You have chosen to go forth and be a part of your journey in your current incarnation *knowing* that this pathway would be offered to you. In the knowing of this, as you claim it, the power – yes, the *power* – will awaken for you. †

It is a matter of realizing your uniqueness, realizing your Authority as a Child of God, putting that into action in your thoughts, words, and deeds. †

To be a part of the work that is at hand is merely to choose it. And, in the choosing, you open yourselves to receive. †

Can you not in this very moment feel the wondrous Love stirring within you, making you feel something wonderful, something that you have known for a long time and had no word to describe? †

You are a precious Child of God. Your claiming of it illuminates you, and this illumination has no limit to its potential. †

In the Knowing, can you find yourself claiming. As you do, the way is open and passable for you. The anchoring within you makes a pathway for the Christ Spirit to be awakened within and to flow through all of you as a wondrous Light offered to all in the Earth. †

What is Truth? The wonder of Truth is the same as all of Consciousness: it is in motion. Truth, as it is perceived in a time in the Earth by individuals, evolves as others see these same circumstances. And even though there are *certainties* regarding certain events, circumstances, scientific *facts*, the beauty of these is their stimulation to seek beyond.

So do not question too long the nature of Truth as you find it expressed without; do rely upon that Truth that is within you: the Knowing that you are His. †

Reach within often. Pause. Ask. Listen. Claim the Peace. Dwell in the Silence. And Love yourselves. †

Allow yourself to Know your Spirit. In the Knowing of your Spirit do you begin the Knowing of God. The enacting of this requires only your choice to do it. †

Send before you the Word of God. As you so do, all will part before you. †

Many of you in the Group have been experiencing extraordinary events. Some of you have noted these. Others of you have only noted them in passing. We would encourage you to recognize subtle shifts in consciousness, events that are occurring that are beyond the ordinary, awakenings in consciousness that have to do with perceptions that are unique or out of the ordinary for you, and the realization of energy shifts that make possible many things that were, just a bit before, much more difficult. †

Let us recognize, again, the Uniqueness that is intended to be the individuality of each Child of God. And as we recognize this, let us hold within a special love of that Uniqueness, a compassion that is of the Christ Himself, that understands the needs, the aspects of growth, the purposes, whether defined or unknown, that seem to be propelling each one towards a destination, known and unknown. †

Let us each, within, claim the glory of God's Light therein ... that which is our very Life. Let us Know this Light, this inner chamber of Holiness, where we, as in the Beginning, are in the present. And let us seek the answer to ourselves, the answer that is the definition, defined in the manner of the Uniqueness that God so Loves us that we have come into Being. †

As we journey forth in the glory of the realization of the beauty that is before us, we look at those things that are as coverings of the beauty of some of our brethren. We grant them forgiveness in the Name of our Lord God, that they might forgive themselves for that which they have, and have not, perpetuated. That they will look about and set Free any burdens that they have or are imposing upon others, knowing that it is God within them that grants them the power of His healing Grace and forgiveness. And as this journey continues on past this good work we do together, let us ever recall that we have paused here in the journey to claim and to offer forgiveness unto all that is. †

Open yourselves. Cast aside that which is the illusion of any need. Rather, seek to open yourself to receive in the peaceful joy as a Child of God. †

Wherever there has been a word that you have taken as an affront to self, look upon that word and the giver of it, that one who has spoken it. Whether it has been appropriate or misguided, it is a burden to both of you for so long as it is held within. If you have an expectation of retribution, of penance, that is required of you or another to you, you are burdened. †

Look upon your brothers and sisters and see them as your Father sees them: beautiful, worthy of your love, as He loves them. †

Seek ye not a temple constructed of the substance of illusion, but seek ye the permanent Light of the temple of God within you, and this will ever serve you. †

The blessings of your loving Father are ever yours. Rise up and go forth, never turning back to gather up the burdens of the past, always looking to the forefront to see the opportunities to give of the wellspring within. As you do, the greater will be given, and you and they will rise up into the fullness of your true heritage. †

Your greatest work begins with you, not the brother or sister to your right or left. It begins with you. †

Some in the realm called Earth know not the Christ; others know of Him and question. Those of you who bear His mark – in other words, who hold a love for Him within your being with all that you are – celebrate them … believer and non-believer, alike. For when the journey in the expression of finiteness in Earth is complete, shall you not stand before the same God? Will you not receive the same opportunities to know the Truth of who you are? †

What is your belief system? To whom do you offer your prayer? Know these things as you begin any good work and affirm clearly that you do not pray to a distant God, but that you move within to the temple that is eternally within you. Stand side by side with God, not beseeching a distant God but as a gift from the God within you.

A belief system is based upon those who hold it and the degree to which they attest to it, but Truth needs none of this, for Truth shall always be, and ever is, within you. †

Gather your Circle with greater intention now than in past. Build your dedication. As you do, another will be set Free, and another, and another. And the Knowing of Freedom will cast rivulets of Light unto the darkness of illusion, that others may take of this Light and it will bloom within them and they will become a source that reaches out beyond them to another, and they to another, and again, and again. Do you see? †

Your gift, as you send it around your Circle, is received and honored by each brother and sister, and as they add their own gift to yours, it increases those rivulets of Light. The power of this lifts you, your entire Group, beyond the illusion, beyond the shadows that would seek to intimidate, or dominate or hold you in the mire of habit. †

Who is it that is blessed by the One God? Someone in a distant land? An individual in a city called New York, or Bombay, or Calcutta? Perhaps in the tiny isle of Bermuda? Who, in all of these lands and so many more, shall hear the call and Awaken? You have the power to send this potential around your Circle, and as it returns to you, it is greatly – majestically greater – a gift returning to *You*, just so as written in the Law. ✝

You are in the midst of a time that has the potential that you have sought for a considerable time, many of you for several lifetimes.

If you look back to a past incident with the intent to cling to this, what shall come of you in the present?

If the one next to you is in a state of Loving Neutrality, celebrating the knowing of what *Is*, holding the expectation of the Promise, and you next to them are clinging to the past, it is better for you to step back than to be a limitation to those who are seeking to set themselves Free. ✝

Truth is simple and beautiful. You, each one, have the power to set yourself Free. Do not fall prey to judging yourself. It is not in the moment that you hold a little thought here or have a little emotion there; but when you come to rest and you move into Oneness with God within you, Free yourself, that you and your Creator can celebrate the beauty of your Uniqueness and the Uniqueness of all of your brethren. ✝

Look to the keys that have been given to you. They were not given idly. Use them. If you find in your day's activities that you are burdened and you find yourself unable to make a space for time with God, use the tools, the keys that have been given to empower you to change this. †

It is said that those who shall rise to the forefront, those who shall be seen in the Light of God's Love, are those who Free themselves to Know Him. Do not take these words to mean you must abandon all and go to the wilderness and be in meditation and prayer. †

Every day of your life is a gift. Every single day is a gift. As it begins, know this, affirm it. Look to the expanse of it, and while there are those things expected of you, those good works you must perform for your body, your physical vehicle, do all these things and whatever else is your measure of need at the side of your Father.

Place your Consciousness of Father by your side by affirming it as you arise. Make it the first activity of your day. Make it the last activity of that day. And make it a joyful pause whenever you can all throughout that day. †

Jesus, when He walked in the Earth, was always joyful and lighthearted. When He was challenged, He did not accept the challenge, but rather, blessed it. Do thou the same. †

When it was asked of Jesus, He did not say to the one asking, "Come here. I will do this or that for you." He asked them to call forth the Presence of God within them with these simple words, *"Do you believe?"*
Immediately, the Path is open, and the Father within the one seeking answers their call. †

The presence of Jesus is the magic of Freedom. We say *magic* because it appears to be an impossibility; therefore, it must be magic. Jesus is the reflection of God within the seeker. Jesus is the Son of God; the seeker is the son or daughter of God. As the seeker opens to ask, they are One. †

You have been sent by the Christ, just as surely as His Disciples of old were sent forth. As you have paused and set yourself Free and set the ideal, the intent, before you of Oneness with God and claimed the Love of God and the Love of your brethren with no boundary, then you are His. And as you go forth in His Name, it shall come to pass in a time that is known by you and He alone that no thing shall be impossible for you in His Name. †

As the Light builds in your current time, many things are awakening ... meditational discoveries, guidance in dreams, the realization in a moment's pause in the sea of beautiful Life in which you exist. These energies are Universal. Those who intend to use them for different purpose, under the Law, have the right to so do. Do not subscribe to their choice. Do not allow their intent to impose upon you to darken the Light of God's Love within. Rather, let this shine forth all the brighter in the face of challenge, in the face of adversity. Remember His words: *"These and greater shall ye do."* †

This is an offering to you all:

The Kingdom of God is before you. Do you wish to seek it? Do you wish to ask? In the Law Universal that embraces the Earth and keeps it from destroying itself, keeps it in a state of potential, you must seek. You must believe. You must set yourself Free. All of these *musts* are meant with the gentle love and compassion of He, Himself. But if you do not see them in the strength of the words that we have used, given to you, will they simply pass you by without such inference, such great emphasis? The emphasis is only present if you are truly seeking; if you are not, well then, do these things if you wish and if not, that's just fine and you will continue on the wheel of life ... free to choose as you wish, free to be limited or unlimited as you choose or submit your choice to others.

But look you carefully: here is the time in the Earth that has been prophesied. And *you have asked. And it is being answered.* †

We love you. Your Creator loves you. Here, in the Consciousness of the All, there is only Love. The truth is that's all there is everywhere. But the wonderful gift of free will that Father gives from the wellspring of His Love for you grants you the right to move into an experience of your creation along with the combined choices of others to experience the depth and breadth of all that is.

The inference is that this is the prime quest. Is it? †

Dwell in the moments surrounded in the Love of God and in the intent, the profound choice, to move into the Sacred Silence and claim the Peace through the pathway of Loving Neutrality. From within this Peace will flow to you God's Love, filling you, guiding you, lifting you up. You have the Authority to choose. You are blessed. †

As it is sought from you, give it, but only insofar as you know this to be a joyful service to your Father that inspires your soul, your Spirit, in the joy of its doing. †

We commend those who are a part of this Group who are gathered about these works presently, and those who may follow. Your dedication and your faith will bring to you the Awakening of your Knowing, of your Seeing. As this is accomplished, you will become Free. †

Know that God's Peace is ever yours, and as we speak a prayer now for you, remember that we speak this prayer at the side of our Lord God in the presence of our Brother the Christ, and the many, many others whose Light is magnificent to behold. We make this prayer, not as a beseechment, but as a statement of truth:

Here before us are the Children of God. We say unto all of Consciousness, honor them.
Here is the Peace of God. We place it before them that they may carry it in all that they are and do. †

[Note: Al, as his Spirit, completes the reading that was being given. For the first time in more than four decades of thousands of readings, he is the one giving the reading.]

ALLEN: I am on a beautiful, green knoll in the Homeland[2].

I am the Completeness of my Being here. Even though there is a form in the Earth that I call my "friend," I am the completeness of my Being.

I see my dear brothers and my dear sisters ... some very clearly, some not quite so. And here is my Hannah, unlimited by thought-forms, claiming her "friend" Susan. Here is my brother Victor contemplating. And right here is my brother James (as I call him), smiling.

And many of the others who are almost always here ... moving about you all, touching you, brushing you off in a manner to take away the things that are limiting or that you no longer need and replacing them with their own Light. It is such a beautiful gift. I think most would weep to see it. It's such a profound act of Love.

I could name more names here, but Zachary and Sarah[3] are suggesting that I do not beyond what I know is appropriate to name. And I understand.

A path has been made for all of you to move here or wherever you would choose, to be with those whom you hold in your heart. (There by the Spring[4] below is Jesus, watching me, listening to me, smiling. And I feel so free, so incredibly peaceful.) And that's my only intent for speaking this way before I return my friend [Earthly Spirit to its form] to the Earth ... just to offer you, every one of you whom I love with all my being, as Father does: the way is open, and here He is. I hope you choose. †

61

These are indeed glorious times in your realm called Earth. Beyond that, these are glorious times in all of existence, for there is the undulation of Spirit combined with the many energies that are a part of the loving souls who comprise the varying groups whose intentions are to gift the glory of God unto all. These are all at a point of intersection, creating the grand opportunity that is present in the Earth. †

You, as the eternal Creation of God, as you gather this Knowing of your Self and Awaken, become a Light for others. It is true, you may not see this from your perception, but then again you may.

The greatest Knowing of this will appear first within you. Be ever vigilant for the shift within, for this will be the indication that you are Awakening, and Knowing, and Seeing. †

Freedom is the presence of the Knowing that you are a Child of God. †

Recognize that You have the Authority, as we have given, to *command* this body, this mind. For You are Spirit eternal, intended to be just as you are by God. †

In those winds of change, the Ocean of Consciousness that swirls about you, the greater you claim the Knowing of your Self to be an eternal Creation of God, the greater is your potential over all those things that are about you in the physical and spiritual sense. †

There is the fullness of God's Compassion, the essence of equality of all that is. This equality could be called the balance of Being. It is the Seeing of this balance that brings the capacity of movement and the expansion of Knowing so much more. †

There are those forces in the balance (often thought of as polarities) that are seeking to dominate the grand energies that are present and to use them for their own intent. As you seek to be Lovingly Neutral, to be in the presence of God's Grace, then be in the state of Peaceful Joy, for this is the expression of God and the balance point. †

In the measurement of Earth time, there are several years remaining for the heightening of the energies to be present[5]. You might think of this as a rich garden prepared for you for eons by beautiful souls who have preceded your journey, whose prayers and love and actions of God's Grace made this garden before you rich and ready to be in receipt of the seeds. The intentions and thought-forms you place before every step of the way – the manner in which you approach one another, the thoughts that precede your words and actions – are the seeds that will be sown.

Knowing this and also knowing that in the sense of the balance scale others are sowing seeds of their own intent, be not idle but active in the expression of your loving Peace – in meditation and prayer and in the focus of the energies that you are perpetuating and sending forth in the ocean of thought that is your realm – by the naming of those in your group, the beautiful Circle of Light. The emphasis upon this is not idle; it is just that valuable that it is worthy of repetition here. †

God's Love is flowing to all of Consciousness ... all that *is* and beyond it. You cannot in the present comprehend, were we to attempt to elucidate it to you what is meant by *beyond it*. Sufficient then, for the present, is to know that there *is* that beyond. †

Life is the Love of God. The life within your body is God's Love for you. Your Spirit is a part of that Light, that Love. That is the River of Life. †

It may seem curious to some that you could have a Spirit that is Conscious and a body that is conscious – and even greater than this – but it is true. †

✿✿✿✿✿✿✿✿✿✿✿

[Note: Because of the highly unusual and profound event that occurred, the following is presented here in its entirety from a reading in this series:]

ZACHARY: We are gathered here in what is called the Homeland beside our brother, the Channel, and several others who are nearby, including myself, Zachary. For those of you who may not know or remember, or who have come along later, I am a brother to the Channel. I dearly love him and he loves me, and I have walked with him in this life and others. I speak on his behalf and he is fully conscious of knowing my speaking:

There is one present in these works who is referred to as Rebochien[6]. He is present here in Spirit form. As I turn to him, he is very bright and alert and of course is completely cognizant of what is transpiring in his body, called Victor in the Earth ... and of course in his mind.

I will loosely translate for him (that is, for Victor's Spirit), for it is not his place to speak in the manner as I do. That would require considerable change here and serves no purpose.

[Victor's Spirit speaking to Victor, incarnated presently in the Earth[7]:]
You have asserted your will with admirable dedication, deliberateness, and, yes, force to cast off

65

what is called in the Earth, dis-ease. You are commended for the power of your will. I am a part of that power, as you are here within me. It is the continued expression of your will, your power, that is present in the current and sustains your body in the manner as it is presently.

ZACHARY: Yes ... a moment, please....
It is pointed out by your spirit that it may seem complicated – the you there/the you here, and my use of terminology in reference. Please forgive and understand that that it's not common for us to use your language, your words, to communicate. It's unnecessary here.
Nonetheless, if you seek a window of opportunity for departure[8], then use your will to do that. He states,

[Victor's Spirit to Victor:] I, your spirit/and you, Victor, are one. This is the glory and celebration that was the intention of my being here with your beloved brother and the Channel of these works; it was not an intent to foretell some doom or something negative but something to be celebratory over[9].
We – you and I, your spirit – have journeyed well in this incarnation. We have completed many good works, and you have reached beyond the veil of separateness to know me in a manner of completeness, as demonstrated by your brother, the Channel, and of course many others.

ZACHARY: Let me pause a moment in speaking to you to point out, over there to the left of the Channel, smiling broadly, is James[10], from the biblical nomenclature (given with humor, as he finds it so in my comments of him).

And down there by the Spring is my beloved sister Marcy[11] who dances about these realms like a beautiful maiden of old. Remarkable how free she is, and as I tell you this, think on it for a moment …

In those moments when her body gave her a signal again that she could be free, she simply chose it. There was no struggle. The efforts of those who sought to keep her in the Earth realm in finite form were very loving and very dedicated, and she has blessed them for it. But as she claimed the opportunity, her will, like yours, is strong … so strong, that she spent little measurable time (as you know it) doing anything other claiming her complete Freedom. Our brother, the Channel, and she have been together many times since her departure from the Earth, and she has passed by here often, and frequently can be seen down there by the collective pool where the Spring waters come to rest.

I tell you this so that you will know it is possible for you to do the same. A moment, please … I will speak with your Spirit a bit.

Very well. He has asked to … asked me to tell you, that is, that your Spirit is curious at your questions.

[Victor's Spirit to Victor:] This is all that you would ask, given the opportunity to communicate in this way? See me here, in the Homeland, your Spirit? I am already here. I am already a part of the group. There is nothing for you to do. It is done.

ZACHARY: And he wishes you to know he gives this with loving humor to you.

[Victor's Spirit to Victor:] The things to watch for[12] are simply this: the body will lovingly give to you (what you might call) signals or notifications

67

that it is ready to be released. The process of releasing the body does not have pain associated with it. It is true that the body may appear to those observers, or any such, to be going through some transitional activities that are defined as pain in the sense of interpretation. But you will not feel this. You will simply rise above the body in a moment of exercising your will.

And in that moment, the glory of God will be known and, so as you choose ... just as we have shown you that Marcy has, so may you in that moment choose whatsoever you wish.

You may return to the embrace of God in the purest sense, as you were in the Beginning but enriched with the journeys you have already taken. Or we may remain here in our completeness with this group. Or you may choose to remain around your mate for a time, or others.

But when the journey is complete, then know this: *I am*.

ZACHARY: I will tell you, as your brother Zachary here, that his intent of stating this is the intent of God, the completeness of His intent for you to *Be*.

✿✿✿✿✿✿✿✿✿✿✿

[This concludes this narrative given for the Group member, Victor. We now return to the format of excerpts.]

The gift of Freedom is the right of choice. The right of choice is invoked by realizing you have the Authority to choose. As you exercise the right of choice, then place before this an intent that is summoned forth from the Center of your Being, where you and God are One.

As the wonder of that choice and the intent that goes before it moves before you, be Free in your interpretation, in your assessment, in your expectation, in your Knowing. For as you begin that journey of your choice and intent, there will be a reaction. You, in your Uniqueness, are impervious to the reaction as you set yourself Free. But if you cling to this little facet here or that little loved aspect there of finiteness, then the challenges, the resistance, the balancing forces, will surely focus upon that, and if possible, your journey will be impeded by it. And though you are impervious, your choice to cling to something limited may have the effect, just so, of limiting you. †

Certainly there is more on any of this, but we would suppose you would need to ask about it, for if you do not, might we not presume it doesn't matter to you? (Lovingly given.) †

Any one of you who might know of these journeys, these words, this message … you can choose to be a part of this. When? Now. In the choosing, you will realize that seeing yourself as limited is a part of the choice of a journey in finiteness. Therefore, the choice must be as simple as choosing to not see it as limited. †

There are many nooks and crannies in the thoughts and machinations that take place in the mind and such of the emotional pool in the Earth. One can delve in these and swim about in the pool of emotion and thought literally for years. Or you can realize who You are, what You are, in this moment. †

You are the Children of God. When you gather together to do the sacred dance of saying the names and gifting one another with Love and Freedom, the Circle of your Presence becomes a power that is placed before the opposing powers to balance them out. This is your right. It is not an infringement on the rights of others because you are not intending an infringement. You are choosing your right to gather together in His Name. And His promise to you – that as you do this, He will be with you – is not idle. This is what is meant by "When those who are His make the way open and passable, He shall return." †

As we look upon you – yes, each one of you in the Group, and greater than you of course – we call out your names. Do you hear us? Do you feel it? †

It is His Glory that surrounds you when you gather together in the Circle. We are always with you, as well. †

Changes are coming and opportunities along with them. Celebrate in the Knowing that this is a joyful journey of choice. †

We thank our brother and his mate, our sister, for their dedication and each of you, as well, for yours.

Pause often to remember one another, just in a sense of joyful peace. And when a thought comes to you to pray for someone or you have a sense of someone's name or their image, pause to celebrate them.

May the Peace of God go before you in all that you are and do. The Love of the Christ is with you. Fare thee well for the present. †

Lord God, as we are gathered together with You and we look upon these beautiful brethren who are seeking in Your Name, we celebrate them each one, in the knowing that, so as we do, the Life that you give us flows through our celebration to embrace them. In the wonder of Life can be found the opportunity to realize that we are Your Children. And as we accomplish this realization, Lord God, it gives us good cause to look about, to reach out, to feel, to know, to experience in every sense that is available to us, the Knowing of Your eternal Presence. As this Knowing becomes complete within us and we see ourselves as eternal Creations of Your Word, your intent, your Love, the glory of that Knowing illuminates all that we are, that we truly become the expression of Your intent of our Being.

Find great joy in the peace and beauty of Pure Being.
✝

On the next page, you will find a list of names of the original members of this group. In the Truth of Oneness, time is not a limitation. You can be a part of this Group's living intent to attain Freedom while yet finite regardless of when you discover this little book. Simply add your name to the list. Our Group has begun to pause in the reciting of our names to include a space for "Those who will follow" … meaning, you.

As best you can, then, recite the names, including yours, daily if possible, which is the general process this group has been using for nearly a year at the time of this publication. In fact, many in the Group recite the names at dawn, twilight, times of challenge, and also spontaneously when the thought of one comes to mind or heart. It has become a source of peace and inspiration, the foundation for our Group intent.

Should you wish to have the complete readings from which these quotes and excerpts have been taken for greater understanding of what the Oneness Group has been about, this set of readings is available on the website as the compilation: "Anchoring the Path."

Know that you are sincerely welcomed, if this calls to you.

The Oneness Group

Aida	James	Marcy
Allen	Janice	Maria
Anja	Jill	Mary
Ann	Jim	Megan
Barbara	Jim	Michael
Barrett	Jimmy	Nancy
Carol	Jochen	Nancy
Charles	Johnstuart	Navin
Christine	Judith	Patrice
Connie	Judith	Patricia
David	Karsten	Remmie
Donald	Katherine	Roxanne
Drew	Ken	Stuart
Ellen	Kendall	Susan
Ernestine	Lennie	Suzanne
George	Linda	Timothy
Grace	Louis	Thomas
Helen	Lunita	Victor
Herk	Lynne	
Jacalyn	Marcelle	

Suggestions from Lama Sing

- Before slumber and upon awakening, pause and remember Who You are. Then, remember the Group.
- Choose *places* throughout your day that you would call Sacred, places where you use your Authority to build a Consciousness. This may be a physical location or it may be in harmony with the movement of the spheres (which you call time) during the day. Two such are native to your realm: sunrise and sunset. As you do this, celebrate your Authority.

If you choose to use sunrise and sunset you could proceed at sunrise with such as, *It is I, (Name) Son or Daughter of God, who greets this day. With the Authority of my Father, I place Joy, Love, and Honor as the Forces that shall move before me in the pathway of this day.*

Then, upon the twilight time, you might say, *I, (Name), give thanks to all that has been in the journey through this day's pathway. I claim the harvest of goodness that has been given to me and place it upon the altar of myself with the full Authority as a Child of God, that these I shall carry with me into my slumber. And, as I serve in realms beyond, this harvest I will give unto any who has need of same.*

You will find yourself guided to use different statements for different purposes.

- Each day, celebrate yourself. When you look into the looking glass, think of Father loving You ... how much He must have wanted You to be, that He would call You forth, give You Life, and the profound treasure chest that You carry within You that is unique to You!

And when You see the face looking back, smiling at You, know that You have made that connection: that You know that You and Father walk together. And celebrate that.

Further Suggestions:

You gathered your Group to form a Circle of loving prayer, and within that intention, you grew to know one another and to love one another in a way that exceeded your previous knowing. This is still growing. When you speak the names of your sisters and brothers, now that you are seeking to set yourself and them Free, we would encourage you to do this with dedication in this manner:

- In the minimum once every seven days, or twice or more if possible, see yourselves gathered together in a beautiful Circle. Pause until you can perceive this as beyond the finiteness of Earth, just beyond the finite expression ... in the realms of spirit. Notice the brilliance you feel from each one as you allow your thoughts to rise above the finite definition into the infinite potential.

- Before you begin speaking names and seeing your brethren, pause and think of your own name. They are all going to speak that name, your name. How will you receive the gifts they will offer you? Will there be any sort of veil? Any thoughts that would be less than the joyful receipt of their offering? If you note these, give them your blessing and set them aside for now, or set them free as is your choice and power to do.

- As you dwell for a few moments upon your name, feel the rising of consciousness within you. Feel the essence, the magic that is the power of your Authority. Choose to be open and to lovingly receive the gifts flowing from Father through your sisters and brothers to you. These are God's gifts flowing through them to you. What a wondrous opportunity! What a beautiful happening for you!

- Having done so to the completeness of your

knowing of it – see, your Knowing of this – begin saying the names, but we encourage you to do so in this way:

- Take a little breath in and speak the name.

- Breathe out a little breath to follow it. As you do, know that you are gifting them with the uniqueness of God that is you, and we and others will do this with and through you.

- In the pause of taking a breath in again, say the next name, and breathe out gently.

As you repeat this again and again for each name, you will begin to feel your Circle move. You will feel the energies heightening, and you will come to know the colors of God's Word: His potentials

Endnotes:

---

[1] The Watch – Is a prayer group with members throughout the world, contributing to countless reported miracles. The prayer Watch began in 1986 as a phone chain, then fax and phone, then email. It is now active and available through the Lama Sing website.

[2] Homeland - This name was given by Susan for purposes of referral to a "place," a consciousness, introduced to us in a reading in 2011: that there are brethren who have since nearly the beginning of time been sustaining the original intent for Earth – a place where all can create with the essences of God and experience those creations in total Freedom.

[3] Zachary and Sarah – Al's guides

[4] The Spring – This was a favorite place of the Essenes during the times Jesus was incarnated and has been, in essence, recreated in the Homeland, also now a favorite gathering place of the Channel, Susan, and other members of the Group, as well as many from the Beyond.

[5] Heightening energies - Great cycles of energy converging until approximately 2018, the potentials offering prophetic opportunity for profound spiritual Awakening.

[6] Rebochien – It was given in the readings about the Essenes that Victor was then known as Rebochien.

[7] Victor's Spirit speaking – In more than 4 decades of previous readings this phenomenon had never occurred, testimony to Victor's dedication to making himself one with his Spirit while yet finite and to the recent accomplishments of Al with his own Spirit.

[8] Window of Departure – Victor had been told several years prior to this reading that he had metastasized cancer. Victor asked Al about "windows" of departure for himself, as Lama Sing had given to Susan's mother for times in which her departure would be one of ease.

[9] Foretelling doom – In a reading prior to this, Al had seen Victor's Spirit, and again several times after that. For one facing a fatal disease, some might have wondered if this event was indicating a departure. Al had explained this was not his assessment, and this reading validated that.

[10] James – Known as Jim W in this Study Group, Jim is now, as of this reading, yet another member whose Spirit Al has seen while on the other side in a readings. This is a different phenomenon than Al seeing the expressions of friends from Earth; this is the Spirit of these friends.

[11] Marcy – Marcy is a member of this Study Group who had a heart attack, surgery, and another heart attack less than 2 weeks prior to this reading. After and since her transition, many in the group reported perceiving her during their prayer works and at other times.

[12] Signs to look for – Included in what Victor had wanted asked were signs of when his departure would be near.

Books by Al Miner & Lama Sing

The Chosen: *Back Story to the Essene Legacy*
The Promise: *Book I of The Essene Legacy*
The Awakening: *Book II of The Essene Legacy*
The Path: *Book III of The Essene Legacy*

In Realms Beyond: *Book I of The Peter Chronicles*
In Realms Beyond: *Study Guide*
Awakening Hope: *Book II of The Peter Chronicles*

How to Prepare for The Journey:
      Vol I. Death, Dying, and Beyond
      Vol II. *The Sea of Faces*

Jesus: *Book I*
Jesus: *Book II*

The Course in Mastery

When Comes the Call

Seed Thoughts
Seed Thoughts to Consciousness

Stepstones: Compilation 1

For a comprehensive list of reading transcripts available,
visit the Lama Sing library at www.lamasing.net

About Al Miner

In 1973, a little more than twenty years after a near-death experience, a chance hypnosis session triggered Al's reconnection to the other side and began his tenure as the channel for the Lama Sing readings.

Since then, over 10,000 readings have been given in a trance state for groups and individuals from around the world, answering questions on a virtually unlimited array of topics. The precision of the information has been substantiated by individuals, professionals, and institutions. Those who have received personal readings continue to refer others to Al's work based on the accuracy and integrity of the information given.

Al has quietly served individuals and groups for over forty years, dedicating his life totally to this work. His focus now is research on Consciousness and its application in daily life. He currently has sixteen books in print.

www.ingramcontent.com/pod-product-compliance
Lightning Source LLC
Chambersburg PA
CBHW060529030426
42337CB00021B/4198